INDIGO GIRLS
BECOME YOU

LYRICS	PIANO VOCAL	GUITAR	
7	8	106	MOMENT OF FORGIVENESS
13	14	110	DECONSTRUCTION
23	24	115	BECOME YOU
31	32	119	YOU'VE GOT TO SHOW
38	39	123	YIELD
47	48	128	COLLECTING YOU
57	58	133	HOPE ALONE
67	68	137	BITTERROOT
76	77	142	OUR DELIVERANCE
83	84	146	STARKVILLE
90	91	151	SHE'S SAVING ME
100	101	155	NUEVAS SENORITAS

ISBN 0-634-04811-2

7777 W. BLUEMOUND RD. P.O. BOX 13819 MILWAUKEE, WI 53213

For all works contained herein:
Unauthorized copying, arranging, adapting, recording or public performance is an infringement of copyright. Infringers are liable under the law.

In Australia Contact:
Hal Leonard Australia Pty. Ltd.
22 Taunton Drive   P.O. Box 5130
Cheltenham East, 3192   Victoria, Australia
Email: ausadmin@halleonard.com

Visit Hal Leonard Online at
www.halleonard.com

MAKING "BECOME YOU"
TREE SOUND STUDIOS, ATLANTA, GA

with Glenn Matullo, Engineer (center)

the band: (L to R) Carol Isaacs, Brady Blade, Emily Saliers, Amy Ray, Clare Kenny

with Russell Carter, manager (2nd from left)

Peter Collins, producer and friend

all photos by Schaune Griffin

CREW

Matt, tour manager, and Michelle, house sound   photo by Amy Ray

Si, monitors   photo by Tal Dayagi

Sulli, guitar tech   photo by Amy Ray

Amy and Emily at 'The Mountain' in Seattle   photo by Debi Lipetz

Dana Powell, RCAM   photo by Amy Ray

photo by Schaune Griffin

IN THE STUDIO

all photos both pages by Schaune Griffin

ON THE ROAD

photo by Tal Dayagi

photo by Tal Dayagi

Haircut time. Tal buzzes Brendan (production manager) backstage   photo by Amy Ray

Crossword puzzle agony   photo by Dana Powell

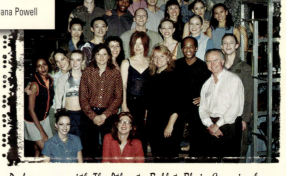
Performance with The Atlanta Ballet. Blair Cunningham, drums (right of Emily)   photo by Schaune Griffin

Radio City   photo by Ross Jones

photo by Tal Dayagi

Photo by Robb D. Cohen

MOMENT OF FORGIVENESS   WORDS AND MUSIC BY AMY RAY

Well I guess that I was lonely, that's why I called you on the phone. 'Cause in a moment of forgiveness, I didn't want to be alone.   And I guess that I was willin,' more than I ever was before, 'cause in a moment of forgiveness, I come a knockin' at your door.   Baby I woke up cryin' last night just to realize that you were gone. Has it been two long years without you? When are you gonna come home? I guess that I was hoping that you'd finally understand, and in a moment of forgiveness, you'd reach out and take my hand.   Now baby I know you're not one for bearing witness. You told me that one wrong move is gonna sell you out. I see that you kept your word and made it harder than it had to be.   Wish I could save you the trouble baby, give you a little peace of mind.   Baby I woke up cryin' last night just to realize that you were gone. Has it been two long years without you? When are you gonna come home? I guess that I was hoping that you'd finally understand, and in a moment of forgiveness, you'd reach out and take my hand.

8

MOMENT OF FORGIVENESS

Words and Music by
AMY RAY

Lead vocal written one octave higher than sung.

© 2002 EMI VIRGIN SONGS, INC. and GODHAP MUSIC
All Rights Controlled and Administered by EMI VIRGIN SONGS, INC.
All Rights Reserved   International Copyright Secured   Used by Permission

Photo by Robb D. Cohen

DECONSTRUCTION   WORDS AND MUSIC BY EMILY SALIERS

We talked up all night and came to no conclusion   We started a fight that ended in silent confusion   And as we sat stuck you could hear the trash truck   Making its way through the neighborhood   Picking up the thrown out different from house to house   We get to decide what we think is no good   We're sculpted from youth, the chipping away makes me weary   And as for the truth it seems like we just pick a theory   The one that justifies our daily lives   And backs us with quiver and arrows To protect openings cause when the warring begins   How quickly the wide open narrows   Into the smallness of our deconstruction of love   We thought it was changing, but it never was   It's just the same as it ever was   A family of foxes came to my yard and dug in I looked in a book to see what this could possibly mean Cause there is fate in the breeze and signs in the trees   Possible tragic events When forces collide with the damage strewn wide   And holes blasted straight through the fence   The sky starts to crash the rain on the roof starts to drumming   And laid out like cash your take on my list of shortcomings   The show starts to close, I know how this goes   The plot a predictable showing   And though it seems grand we're just one speck of sand   And back to the hourglass we're going   Back to the smallness of our deconstruction of love   We thought it was changing, but it never was Our deconstruction of love

Photo by Schaune Griffin

BECOME YOU   WORDS AND MUSIC BY AMY RAY

I heard you sing a rebel song, sung it loud and all alone. We can't afford the things you save, we can't afford the warranty. I see you walking in the glare down the county road we share. Our southern blood, my heresy, damn that ol' confederacy.   It took a long time to become the thing I am to you. And you won't tear it apart without a fight, without a heart.   I'm sorry for what you have learned, when you feel the tables turn. To run so hard in your race, now you find who set the pace. The landed aristocracy exploiting all your enmity. All your daddies fought in vain, leave you with the mark of Cain.   It took a long time to become the thing I am to you. And you won't tear it apart without a fight, without a heart. It took a long time to become you, become you.   The center holds, so they say, it never held too well for me. I won't stop short for common ground that vilifies the trodden down. The center held the bonded slave for the sake of industry. The center held the bloody hand of the executioner man.   It took a long time to become the thing I am to you. And you won't tear it apart without a fight, without a heart. It took a long time to become you, become you.

Photo by Dana Powell

YOU'VE GOT TO SHOW   WORDS AND MUSIC BY EMILY SALIERS

Yes it's true I've gotten very moody over you Don't think I don't sense your caution way across the room Or across the phone lines, big black ocean, or conversation brief We can't find a clear connection, and I can't get relief   Why don't we both agree we're both afraid and too afraid to say If I say count to three and move toward me, would you meet me half the way There are a thousand things about me I want only you to know But I can't go there alone, you've got to show   While you occupy me I command my dreams each day To bring you in me even thinly as the morning chases you away I half believe if I just picture us we will come true Wishful thinking or my dreams sinking half depends on you Show me you are fully alive   If you want to fly you take this dive If you want to kiss, kiss for real I'll give you back everything you feel   Drive in space that peaceful place You'd be my secret sharer Front and back and all around the thin margin of error Move too fast or move too slow or somewhere in between Navigate the perfect distance so your getaway is clean   Why don't we both agree we're both afraid and too afraid to say If I say count to three and move toward me would you meet me half the way There are a thousand things about me I want only you to know But I can't go there alone, you've got to show

YOU'VE GOT TO SHOW

Words and Music by
EMILY SALIERS

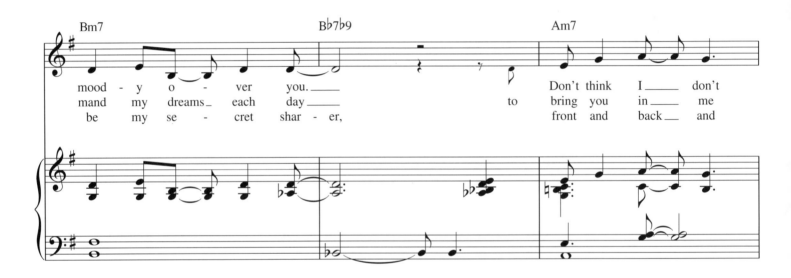
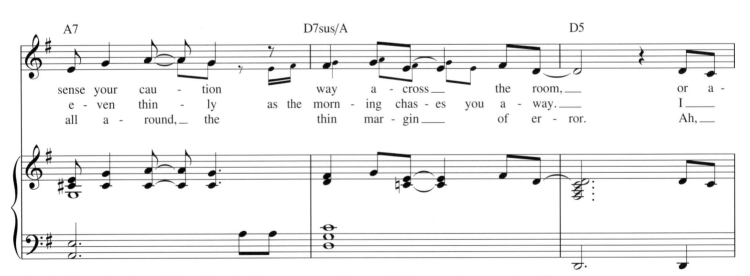

Yes, it's true I've gotten very
While you oc-cu-py me I com-
Drive in space, that peace-ful place, you'd

mood-y o-ver you. Don't think I don't
mand my dreams each day to bring you in me
be my se-cret shar-er, front and back and

sense your cau-tion way a-cross the room, or a-
e-ven thin-ly as the morn-ing chas-es you a-way. I
all a-round, the thin mar-gin of er-ror. Ah,

Original key: E♭ minor. This edition has been transposed up one half-step to be more playable.
* Chord symbols reflect guitar chord voicings.

© 2002 EMI VIRGIN SONGS, INC. and GODHAP MUSIC
All Rights Controlled and Administered by EMI VIRGIN SONGS, INC.
All Rights Reserved   International Copyright Secured   Used by Permission

Photo by Schaune Griffin

YIELD   WORDS AND MUSIC BY AMY RAY

I was downstairs in the green room waiting for you to appear. I said hello to your family, I said hello to your friends, I said hello to this situation that never yields.   Now it's easy for me to tell you that my love for you is real. I once stumbled on these feelings, I once stumbled on these words, something you'll never stumble on dear.   Oh you were so baroque all of those words, just to tell me no. You were so soft spoken with all of the others who said you weren't broken, they just let you go.   When you're three days down the highway and you're looking like I feel; if it takes a lot to keep it going, if it takes a lot to keep it real, take some time for yourself and learn to yield.

Photo by Schaune Griffin

COLLECTING YOU   WORDS AND MUSIC BY EMILY SALIERS

I could paint you in the dark Cause I've studied you with hunger like a work of art These are very secret days I collect my information then I stowe it all away   Call me when you breeze through to your appointments The work you do Call me, I'm collecting you   The pleading prayer and hairshirt sting My hairtrigger love and faulty spring Motivation smokes a name, but I don't like that smell applied to me so blindly just the same   Call me when you breeze through to your appointments the work you do Call me I'm collecting you   Turning up my collar to an unseasonal chill you ask a favor, you know I will The rain comes a surprise we fly across the railroad ties I feel the danger the foolish thrill oh yes I will What it will or won't be then The shutter pre development the ink full in the pen Mind the mind's eye's trickery You might picture killer beautiful much more than it might be   Call me tell me what you're up to what you'll do Call me I'm collecting you   I would be foolish to think that I could turn it off and stay alive The way I live when you switch on hand on the dimmer, give me just a glimmer Give me just a shadow hope around the edges, agony and rapture forever uncaptured   Take these secrets to your grave Drug across your landscape and buried in your cave You're piling up and out of sight But trying to add it up just feels like counting shades of light   Call me tell me what you're up to what you'll do Call me I'm collecting you   Hang it in my window let it complicate my view The separation the glass of you But I can paint this picture any way that I see fit The art of pain the subject sits unmoved

COLLECTING YOU

Words and Music by
EMILY SALIERS

Photo by Schaune Griffin

HOPE ALONE   WORDS AND MUSIC BY EMILY SALIERS AND ANNIE ROBOFF

Let's not drag this out, everything's in motion Though I've only ever loved you kind and with devotion I remember when I met you and even from the start I thought one day you'd probably just come home and break my heart   It's funny what you know and still go on pretending With no good evidence you'll ever see that happy ending   You were looking for your distance and sensing my resistance you had to do your will I had to learn the hard way We were just an empty dream too big for hope alone to fill I know I'm a dreamer, so I'll give you that Still I hope I'm more than just a place you laid your hat You're a land of secrets, its only citizen And though I paid my dues I was never allowed in   And so I am a stranger but especially today As I get sad and lonely and you get your way   You were looking for your distance and sensing my resistance you had to do your will I had to learn the hard way We were just an empty dream too big for hope alone to fill   Holding out for change I know we never stood a chance So I could only wait and watch you slip right through my hands

HOPE ALONE

Words and Music by EMILY SALIERS
and ANNIE ROBOFF

* *Lead vocal written one octave higher than sung.*

© 2002 EMI VIRGIN SONGS, INC., GODHAP MUSIC, ALMO MUSIC CORP. and ANWA MUSIC
All Rights for GODHAP MUSIC Controlled and Administered by EMI VIRGIN SONGS, INC.
All Rights for ANWA MUSIC Controlled and Administered by ALMO MUSIC CORP.
All Rights Reserved   International Copyright Secured   Used by Permission

* Gtr.2 plays (Fmaj7).

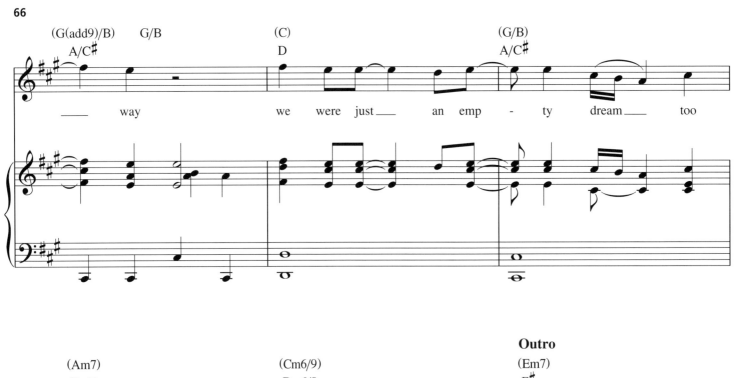
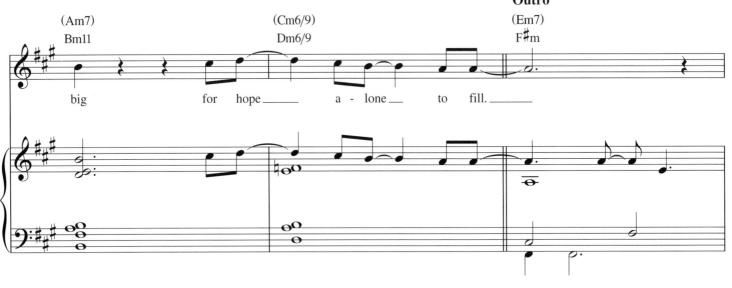
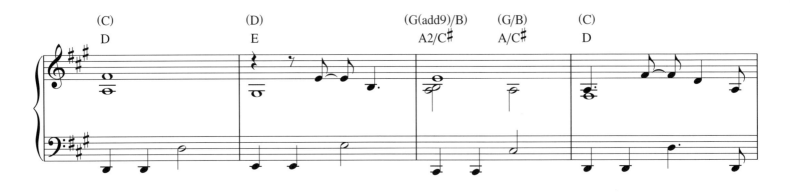
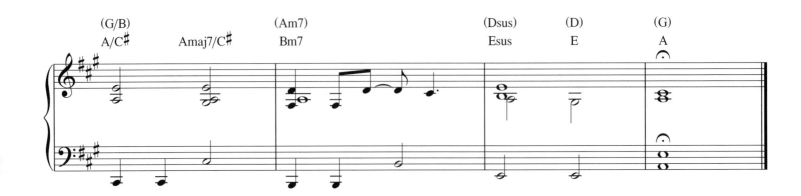

Photo by Schaune Griffin

BITTERROOT   WORDS AND MUSIC BY AMY RAY

Tonight I'll be sleeping on the mountain top, I got a billion stars for my witness. In the morning I'll go down and the sun comes up, I'll take a drink from the Bitterroot River.   Have you been lonely? Yes, I've been lonely. I've been lonely, too.   Tonight I'll be sleeping on the mountain top, I got a billion stars for my witness. In the morning I'll go down and the sun comes up, I'll take a drink from the Bitterroot River.   Have you been travelin'? Yes, I've been travelin.' I've been travelin,' too. Tonight I'll be sleeping on the mountain top, I got a billion stars for my witness. In the morning I'll go down and the sun comes up, I'll take a drink from the Bitterroot River.

BITTERROOT

Words and Music by
AMY RAY

*Lead vocal written one octave higher than sung.

© 2002 EMI VIRGIN SONGS, INC. and GODHAP MUSIC
All Rights Controlled and Administered by EMI VIRGIN SONGS, INC.
All Rights Reserved   International Copyright Secured   Used by Permission

* Chord symbols reflect guitar chord voicings.

Photo by Tal Dayagi

OUR DELIVERANCE   WORDS AND MUSIC BY EMILY SALIERS

Now we can say that nothing's lost and only change brings 'round the prophecy Where now it's melting, the solid frost was once a veil on greener landscapes we would see   Beneath my surface the water's heating And steam comes up and out the tears you see me shine For every strange and bitter moment there was never a better time   For every pleasure exacts its pain How you hurt me how you were good to me Beneath my window a mournful train that makes me smile at my bad poetry Beneath my surface a song is rising It may be simple while it hides its true intent We may be looking for our deliverance but it has already been sent   It's in the nightfall when the light falls And what you've seen isn't there anymore It's in our blind trust that love will find us Just like it has before   They're sending soldiers to distant places X's and O's on someone's drawing board Like green and plastic but with human faces And they want to tell you it's a merciful sword   But with all the blood newly dried in the desert Can we not fertilize the land with something else There is no nation by god exempted Lay down your weapons and love your neighbor as yourself   In the nightfall when the light falls And what you've seen isn't there anymore It's through our blind trust that love will find us Just like it has before

OUR DELIVERANCE

Words and Music by
EMILY SALIERS

Intro
Moderately slow

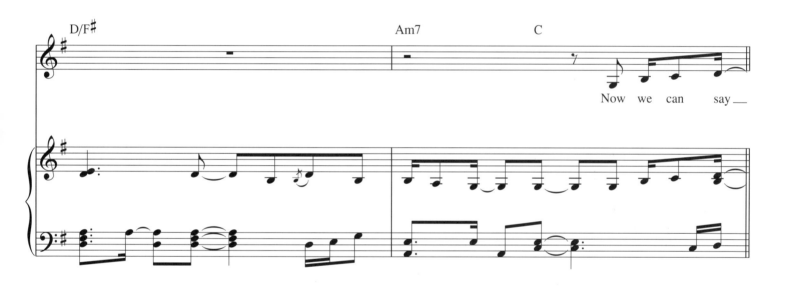

Now we can say_

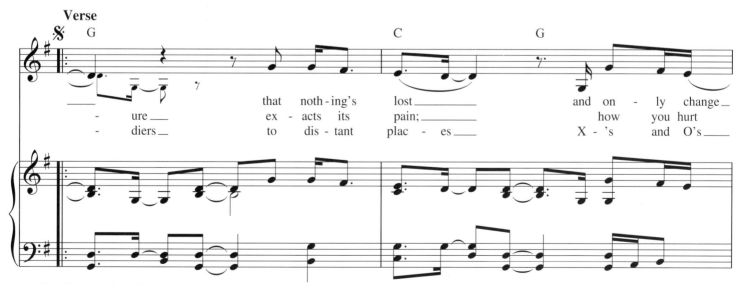

Verse

-ure___ex- acts its pain;___ how you hurt
that noth-ing's lost___ and on- ly change_
-diers___ to dis- tant plac- es___ X-'s and O's___

* Chord symbols reflect guitar chord voicings.

© 2002 EMI VIRGIN SONGS, INC. and GODHAP MUSIC
All Rights Controlled and Administered by EMI VIRGIN SONGS, INC.
All Rights Reserved International Copyright Secured Used by Permission

* 2nd & 3rd times, Bouzouki & mandolin play Dsus2.

* Bouzouki & mandolin play G.

* Bouzouki & mandolin play Dsus2.
** Bouzouki & mandolin play G.

* Bouzouki & mandolin play G.
** Mandolin plays Dsus2.

Photo by Tal Dayagi

STARKVILLE   WORDS AND MUSIC BY AMY RAY

If you were here in Starkville, the townie boys would love the way you stare. If you were here in Starkville, the local girls, they wouldn't have a prayer. I spent a reckless night inside the wonder of your everlasting charm, now I'm haunted by geography, and the flora and the fauna of your heart. At the dawning of some road-worn day, I called you on a whim just to say, "The morning birds are singing," but I could not do them justice, so I hung up and fell back to sleep.   I'm in love with my mobility, but sometimes this life can be a drag; like when I noticed your nobility and how my leaving only held you back. I remember one occasion—you were drinking—when you asked me to the coast, but I was hell-bent on agony back then, so I missed the boat.   At the dawning of a road-worn day, I called you on a whim just to say, "My regrets become distractions when I cannot do them justice," then I hung up and fell back to sleep.   When I was down in Starkville, I was hiding out inside some Comfort Inn from a local gang of troubadors, when the homecoming queen—she come riding in. I slipped out of my room into the rain I went running for my health, the headlights turned to moonlight, and finally I was running by myself. At the dawning of this road-worn day, I call you on a whim just to say, "The morning birds are singing."

STARKVILLE

Words and Music by
AMY RAY

*Lead vocal written one octave higher than sung.
Original key: E♭ minor. This edition has been transposed up one half-step to be more playable.

© 2002 EMI VIRGIN SONGS, INC. and GODHAP MUSIC
All Rights Controlled and Administered by EMI VIRGIN SONGS, INC.
All Rights Reserved   International Copyright Secured   Used by Permission

* 2nd time, Gtr.1 plays Em7.
** 2nd time, Gtr.1 plays C type2.
*** 3rd time, Gtr.1 plays E5 instead of Em till Pre-Chorus.

* 2nd time, Gtr.1 plays Em7.
** 2nd time, Gtr.1 plays C^{type2}.
*** 2nd time, Gtr.1 plays C6/9.

Photo by Tal Dayagi

SHE'S SAVING ME   WORDS AND MUSIC BY EMILY SALIERS

We were sitting 'round a dying fire, somebody lit incense somebody lit a cigarette and passed the bottle around   It was just strawberry season, backbreaking pickers in the patches everything's burning down to ashes and down to the ground   She's saving me I don't even think she knows it It's a strange way to show it as distant as last night's dream unravels She's saving me I'm a very lost soul I was born with a hole in my heart The size of my landlocked travels   I try to put it aside but it's too much bigger than me there's a big brown hawk in the tree   Lighting and leaving   There's tea leaves tossing, heads up pennies in my pocket, dead star like a rocket, the arc of my grieving   She's saving me I don't even think she knows it It's a strange way to show it as distant as last night's dream unravels She's saving me I'm a very lost soul I was born with a hole in my heart The size of my landlocked travels   The sky pours out biblical rain Then days so still the beauty gives you pain The heatwave kills the green and she remains unseen But colors up my dreams with all things blooming   This is not all there is it's not a kingdom it's not an angry god It feels like her It feels like no fear, it feels like no doubt, it feels like inside out The ashes stir   She's saving me I don't really think she knows it It's a strange way to show it as distant as last night's dream unravels She's saving me I'm a very lost soul I was born with a hole in my heart as wide as my landlocked travels

SHE'S SAVING ME

Words and Music by
EMILY SALIERS

* Chord symbols reflect guitar chord voicings.

© 2002 EMI VIRGIN SONGS, INC. and GODHAP MUSIC
All Rights Controlled and Administered by EMI VIRGIN SONGS, INC.
All Rights Reserved   International Copyright Secured   Used by Permission

Photo by Schaune Griffin

NUEVAS SENORITAS   WORDS AND MUSIC BY AMY RAY
Well, we blew off immigration, the moon was sitting high, as we drove from the Lacandon into Comitan. Gloria was singing and Cecilia closed her eyes, and I saw them drifting out over the night sky. Nuevas Senoritas, are you gone to brighter days? Have you found your greener valleys and the place where your heart stays?   I'm heading back to the flatlands and you're heading up to the hills. The rain brings you home in the middle of July.   I guess I just got lonesome when I think about how you feel, with six months gone and no one to dry your eyes.   Nuevas Senoritas, are you gone to brighter days? Have you found your greener valleys and the place where your heart stays?

NUEVAS SEÑORITAS

101

Words and Music by
AMY RAY

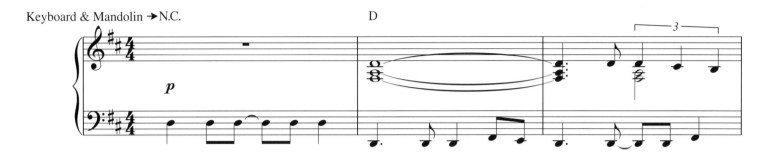
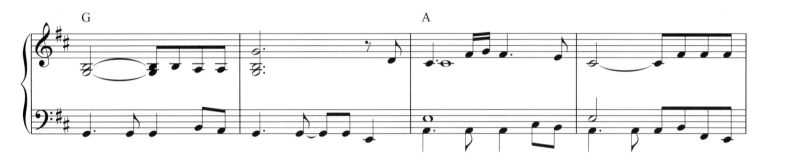
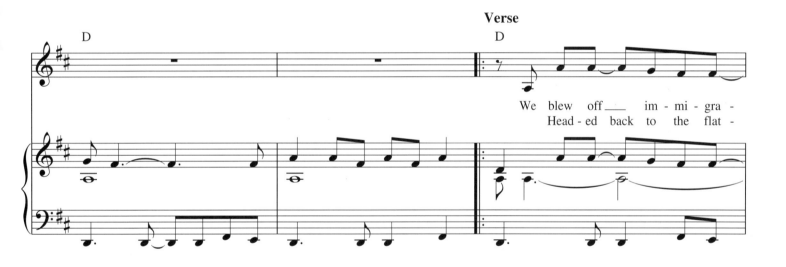
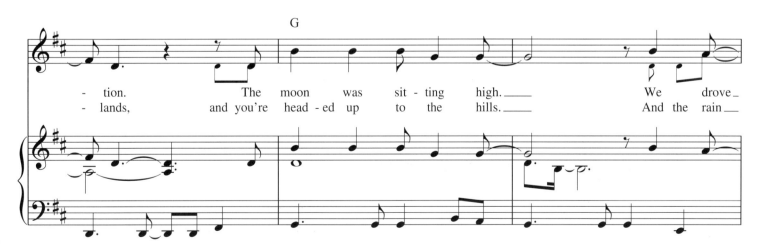

We blew off im-mi-gra-
Head-ed back to the flat-

-tion. The moon was sit-ting high. We drove
-lands, and you're head-ed up to the hills. And the rain

© 2002 EMI Virgin Songs, INC. and GODHAP MUSIC
All Rights Controlled and Administered by EMI VIRGIN SONGS, INC.
All Rights Reserved International Copyright Secured Used by Permission

GUITAR SECTION

GUITAR

106	**MOMENT OF FORGIVENESS**
110	**DECONSTRUCTION**
115	**BECOME YOU**
119	**YOU'VE GOT TO SHOW**
123	**YIELD**
128	**COLLECTING YOU**
133	**HOPE ALONE**
137	**BITTERROOT**
142	**OUR DELIVERANCE**
146	**STARKVILLE**
151	**SHE'S SAVING ME**
155	**NUEVAS SENORITAS**

We have included this special GUITAR SECTION so you can play exactly what Amy and Emily played on *Become You* – the correct tunings, capo placements and chord voicings. We have even included their mandolin and bouzouki parts. At the beginning of each song is a tuning legend. It is here that we list capo locations and/or altered tunings.

For example, in the song "Moment of Forgiveness," guitar one is in standard tuning and guitar two is capoed at the seventh fret. All of the appropriate chord diagrams for each song are listed below the song title.

"Yield," "Our Deliverance" and "Nuevos Señoritas" all contain bouzouki and/or mandolin parts. If you don't own a bouzouki or mandolin, try tuning the first four strings of your guitar to the pitches indicated. Here's how: your high E string will remain tuned to E. Lower the pitch of your second string a whole step to A (it should sound like your third string fretted at the second fret). Next, tune your third string down 2 1/2 steps to D (it should now be the same pitch as your fourth string open). Tune your fourth string down 3 1/2 steps to G (it should now sound like your sixth string fretted at the third fret). If you have a cutaway on your guitar, try capoing at the twelfth fret. Your guitar will sound even more like a mandolin!

Each transcription has been divided into its component sections. These sections are labeled "Intro," "Verse," "Chorus," etc. Once you have learned how to play each section of a particular song, go to the front half of this book to the actual song. You will notice that the songs contain the same section names as those labeled in the GUITAR SECTION. By following the roadmap of sections, you can play the complete song just like it is on the CD.

Have fun!

MOMENT OF FORGIVENESS
(Guitar Parts)

Words and Music by Amy Ray

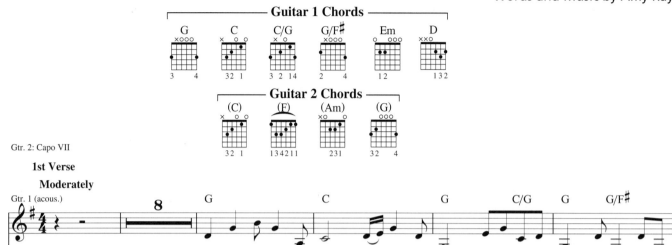

Gtr. 2: Capo VII

1st Verse
Moderately

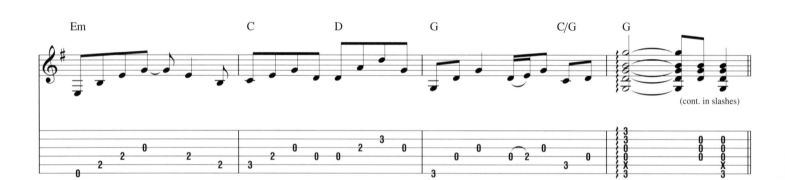

1st Chorus
Sample strum pattern

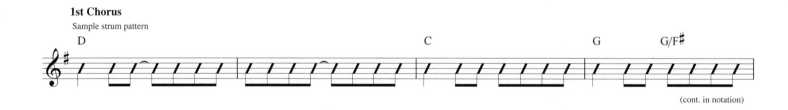

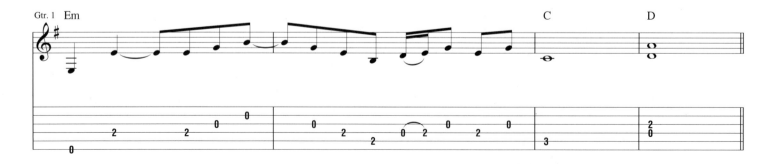

© 2002 EMI VIRGIN SONGS, INC. and GODHAP MUSIC
All Rights Controlled and Administered by EMI VIRGIN SONGS, INC.
All Rights Reserved   International Copyright Secured   Used by Permission

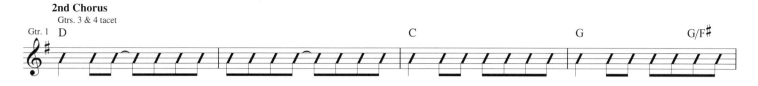

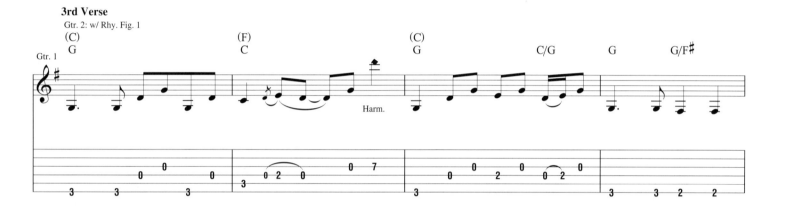
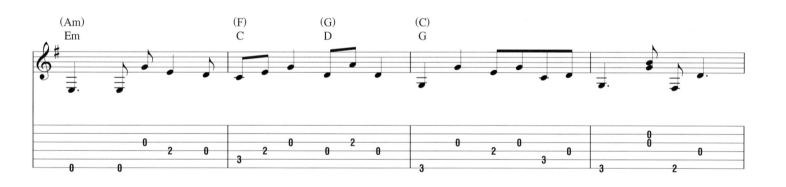
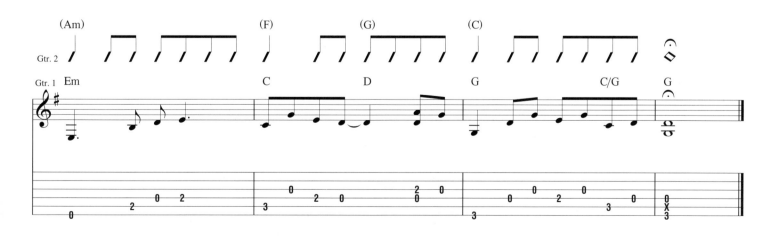

DECONSTRUCTION
(Guitar Parts)

Words and Music by Emily Saliers

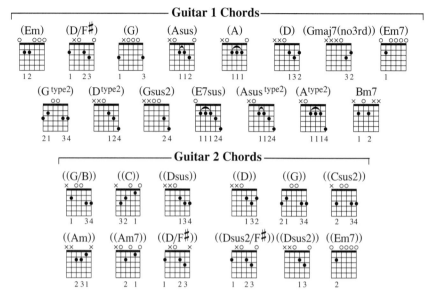

Gtr. 1: Capo VII
Gtr. 2: Capo II

Intro

Moderately slow in "2"

1st Verse

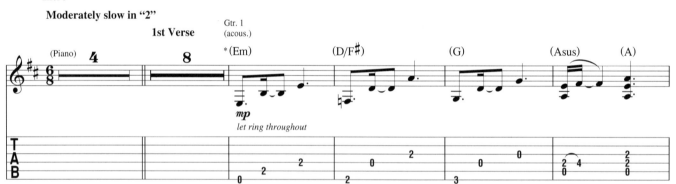

*Symbols in single parentheses represent chord names respective to capoed Gtr. 1. Capoed fret is "0" in tab.

**Symbols in double parentheses represent chord names respective to capoed Gtr. 2. Capoed fret is "0" in tab.

© 2002 EMI VIRGIN SONGS, INC. and GODHAP MUSIC
All Rights Controlled and Administered by EMI VIRGIN SONGS, INC.
All Rights Reserved   International Copyright Secured   Used by Permission

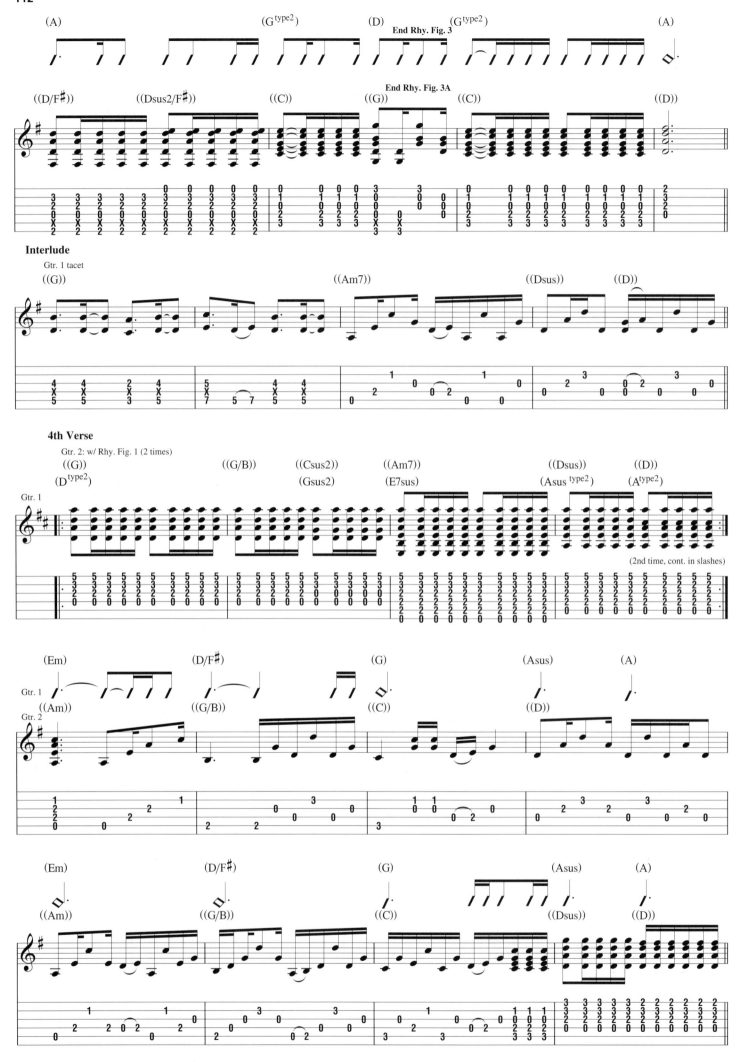

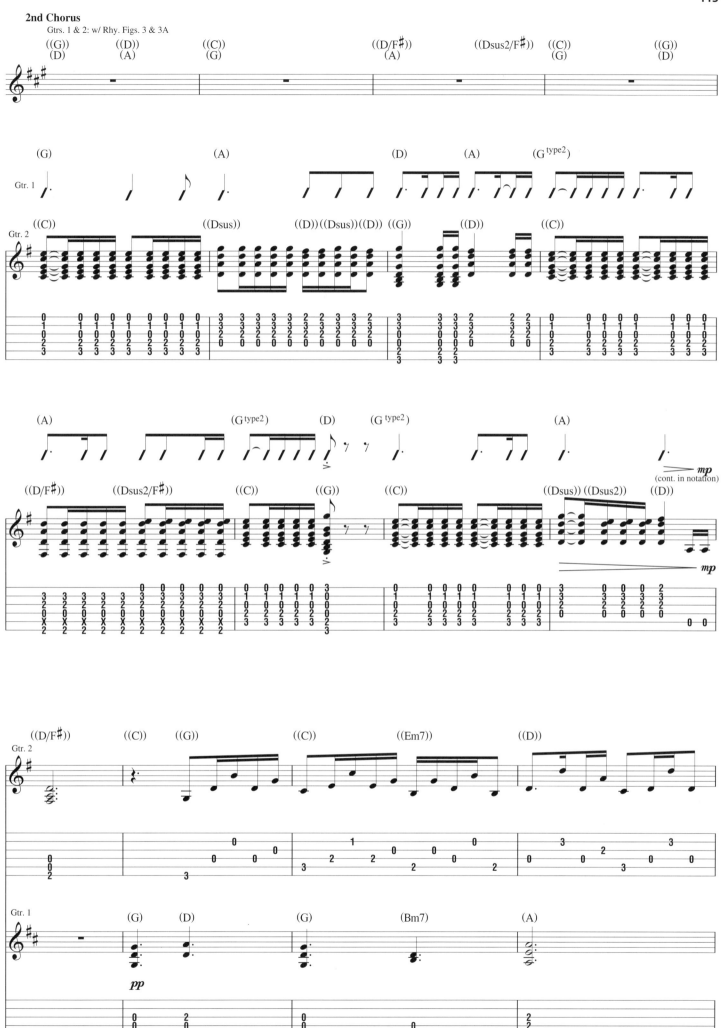

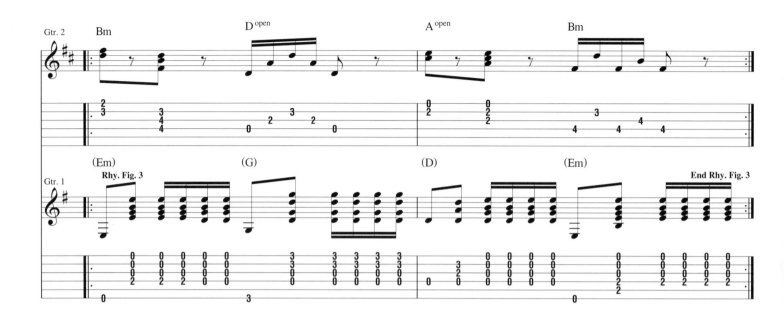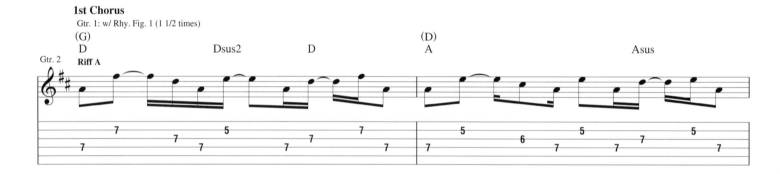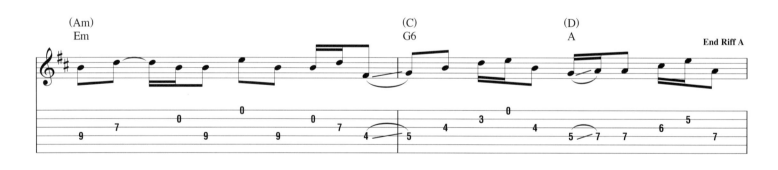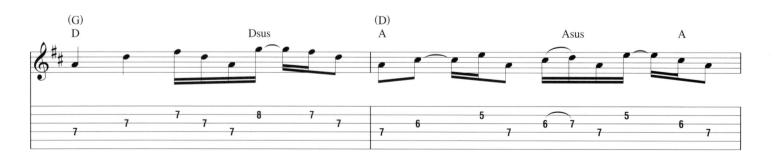

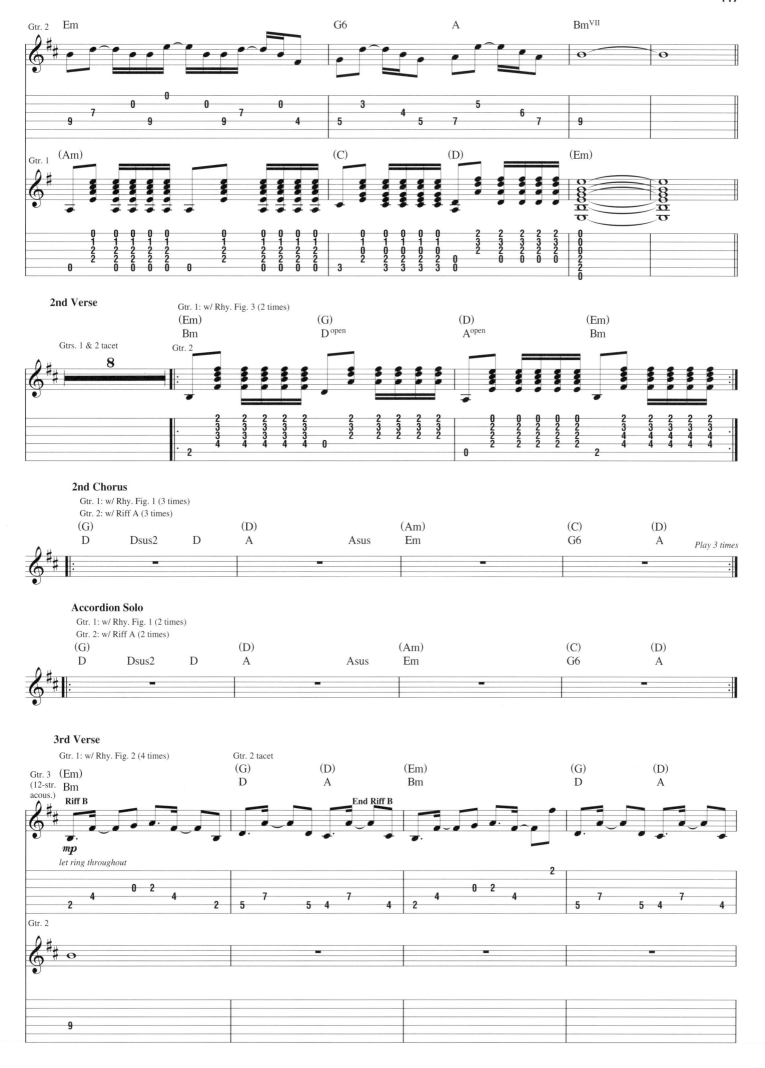

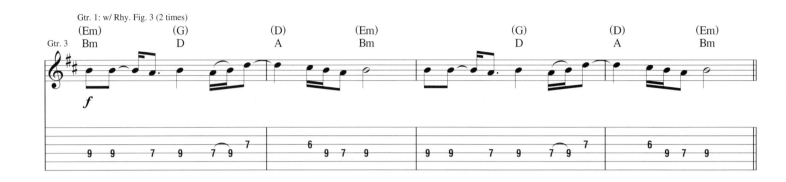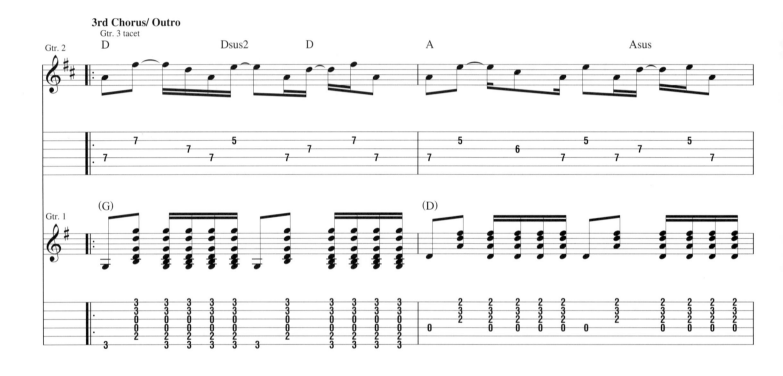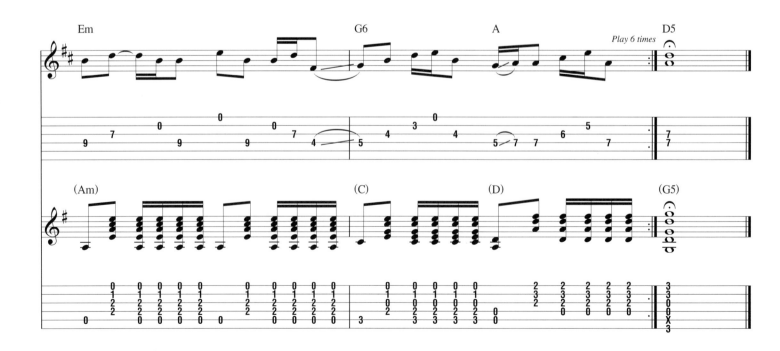

YOU'VE GOT TO SHOW
(Guitar Parts)

Words and Music by Emily Saliers

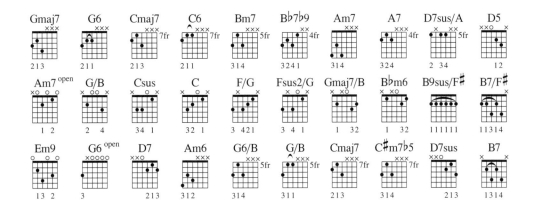

Tune down 1/2 step:
(low to high) E♭-A♭-D♭-G♭-B♭-E♭

1st Verse
Moderately

Gtr. 1 (acous.)

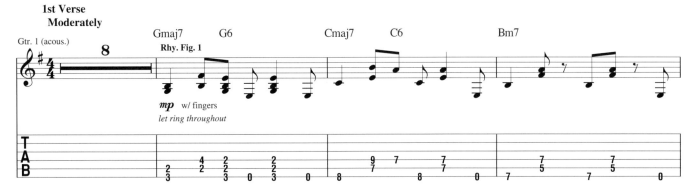

mp w/ fingers
let ring throughout

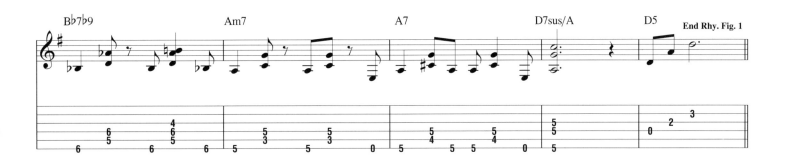

Chorus

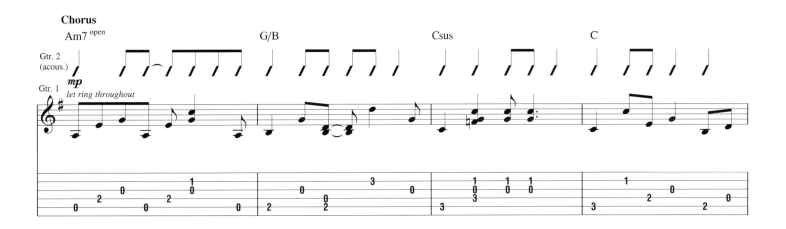

© 2002 EMI VIRGIN SONGS, INC. and GODHAP MUSIC
All Rights Controlled and Administered by EMI VIRGIN SONGS, INC.
All Rights Reserved   International Copyright Secured   Used by Permission

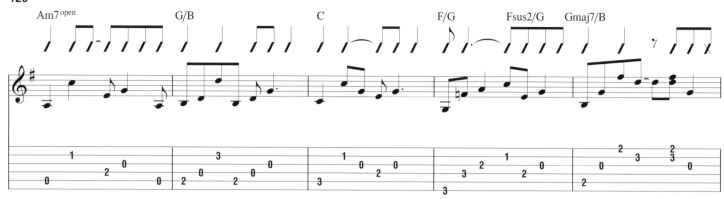
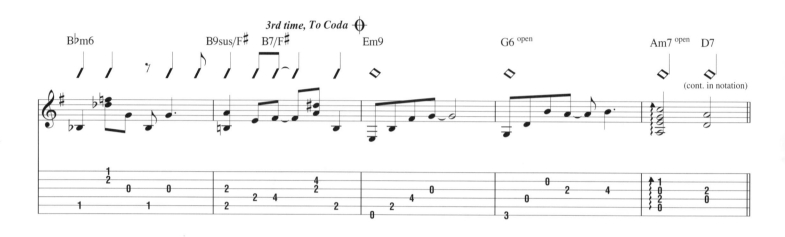
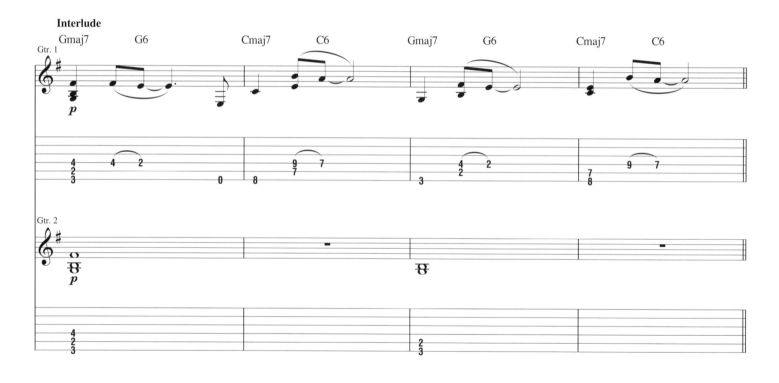
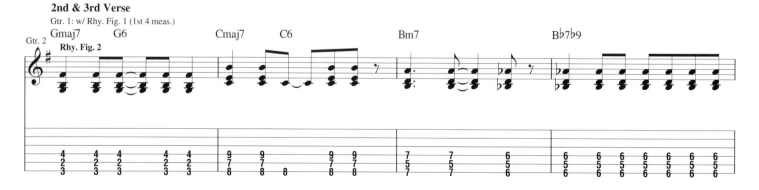

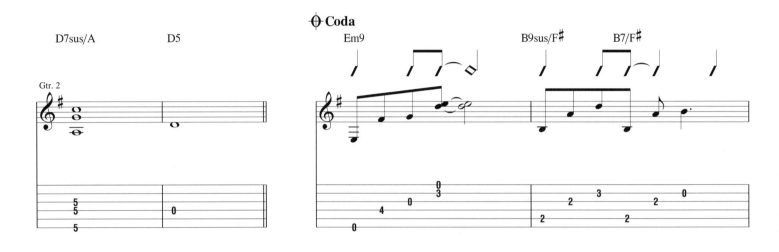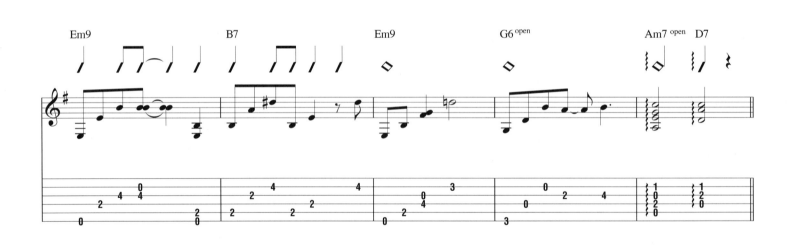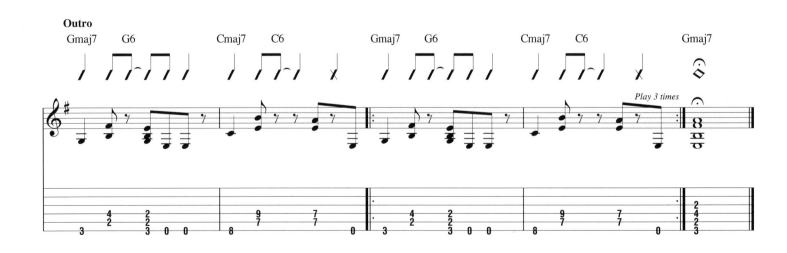

YIELD
(Mandolin & Guitar Parts)

Words and Music by Amy Ray

* Symbols in parentheses represent chord names respective to capoed guitar/ mandolin. Capoed fret is "0" in tab.

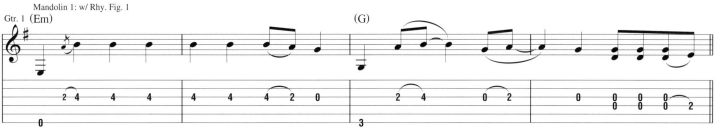

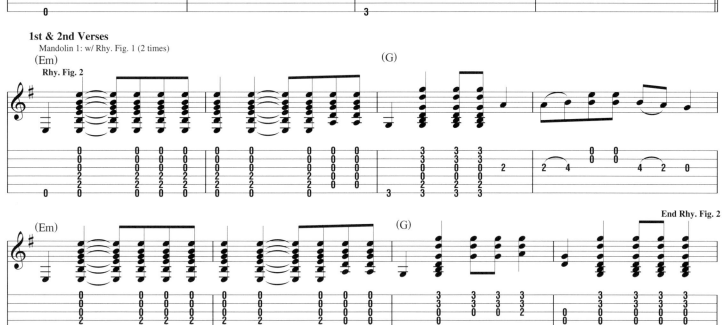

© 2002 EMI VIRGIN SONGS, INC. and GODHAP MUSIC
All Rights Controlled and Administered by EMI VIRGIN SONGS, INC.
All Rights Reserved   International Copyright Secured   Used by Permission

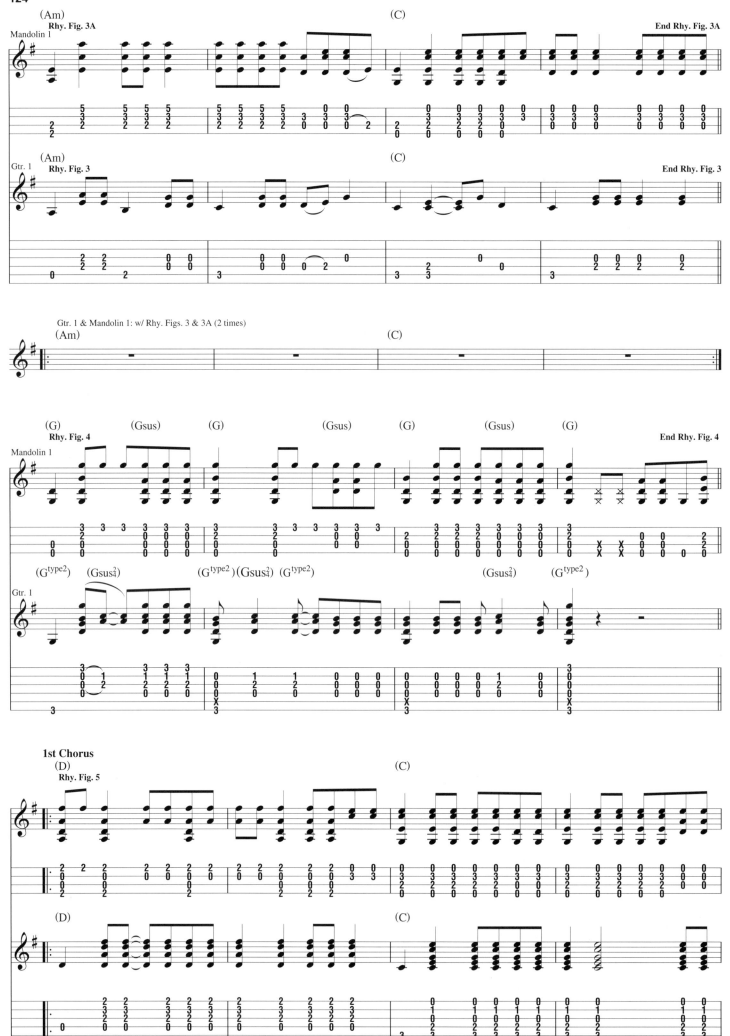

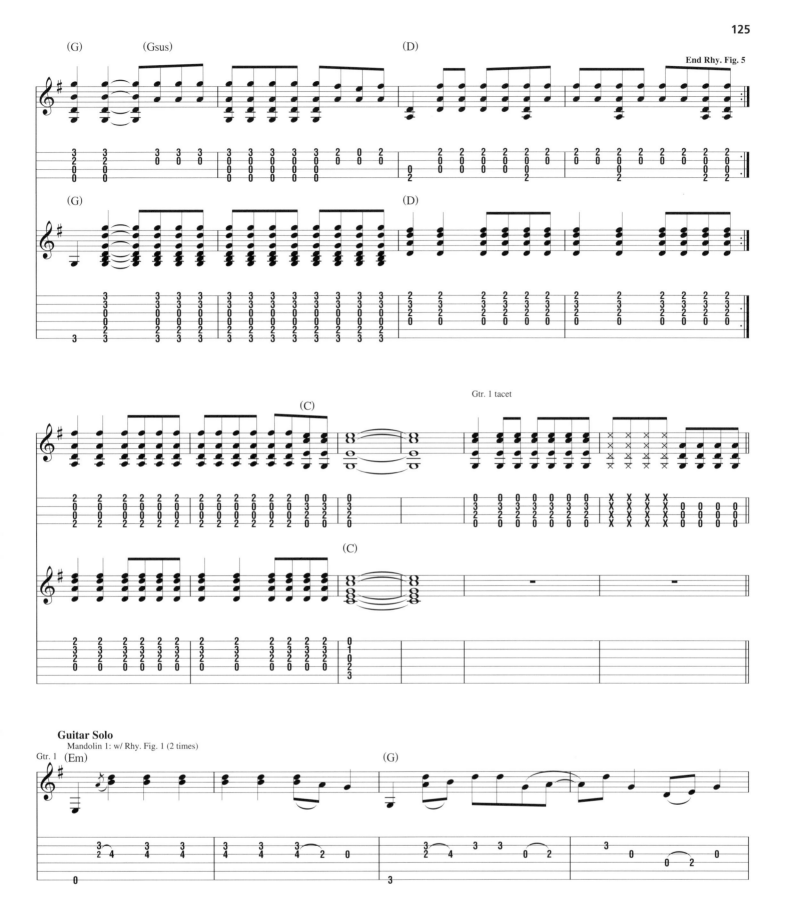
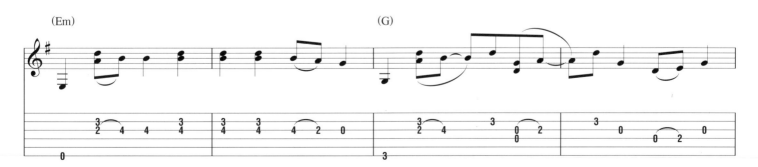

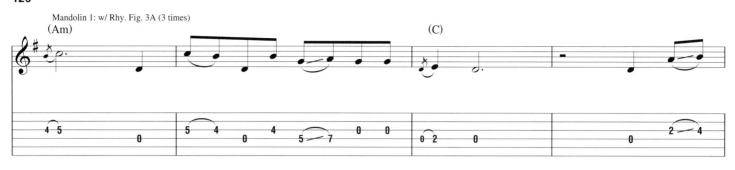
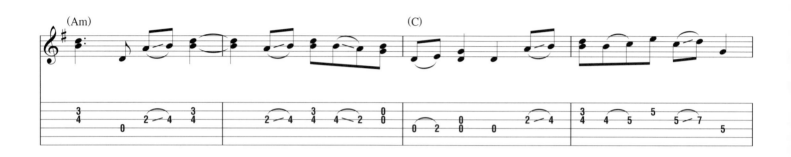

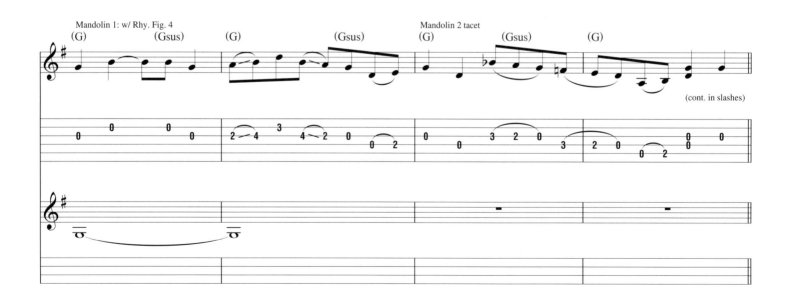

COLLECTING YOU
(Guitar Parts)

Words and Music by Emily Saliers

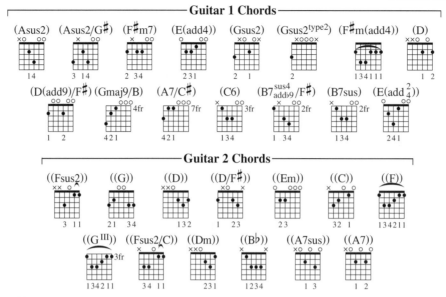

Gtr. 1: Tuning, Capo II:
(low to high) E-A-D-G-A-E

Gtr. 2: Capo IV

Intro
Moderately

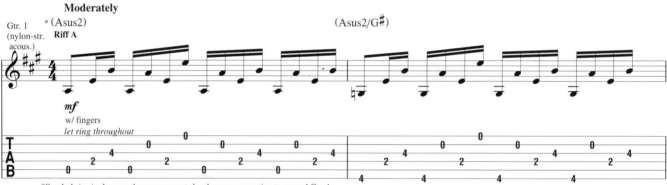

*Symbols in single parentheses represent chord names respective to capoed Gtr. 1.
Capoed fret is "0" in tab.

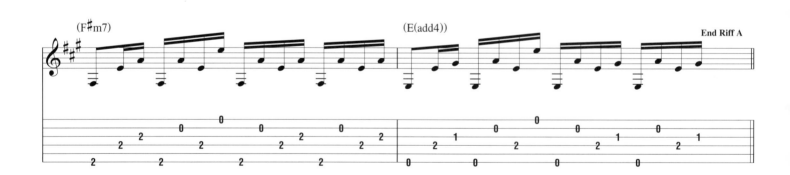

1st Verse
Gtr. 1: w/ Riff A (2 times)

© 2002 EMI VIRGIN SONGS, INC. and GODHAP MUSIC
All Rights Controlled and Administered by EMI VIRGIN SONGS, INC.
All Rights Reserved   International Copyright Secured   Used by Permission

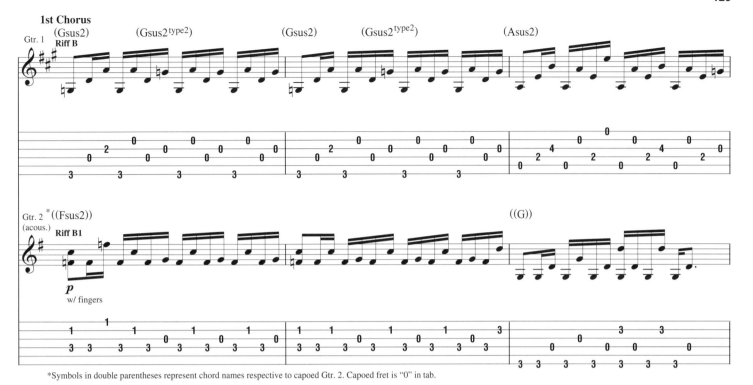
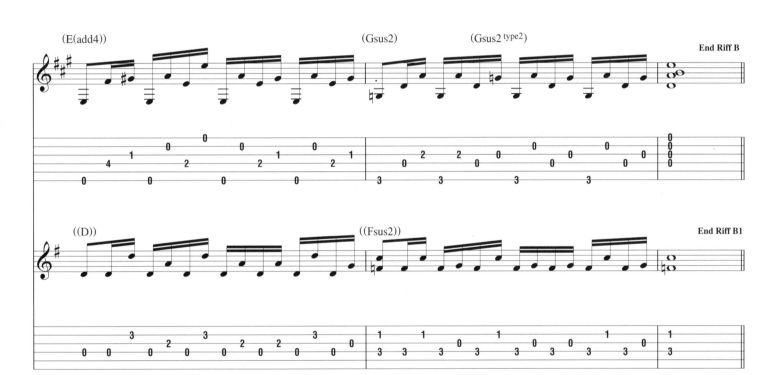

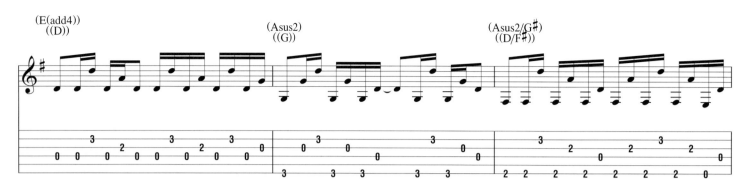
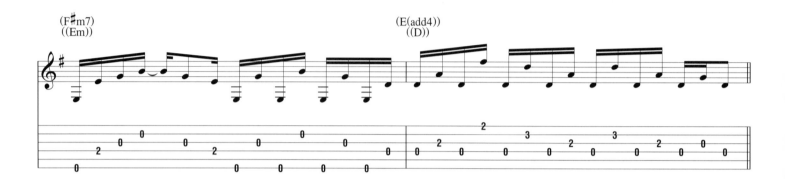
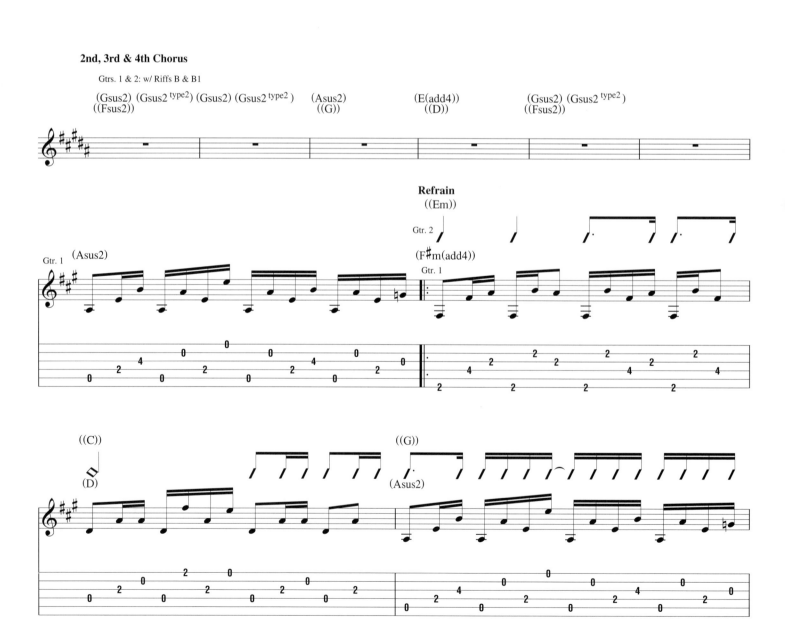

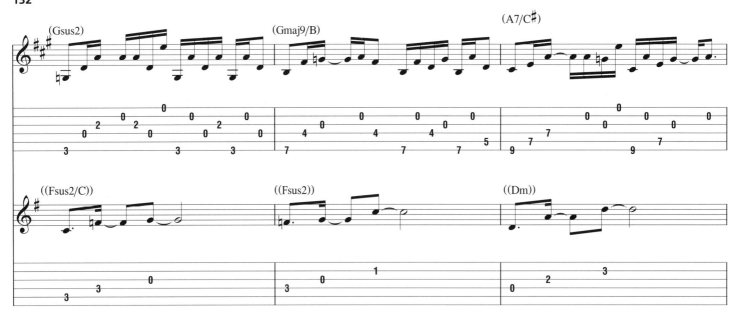
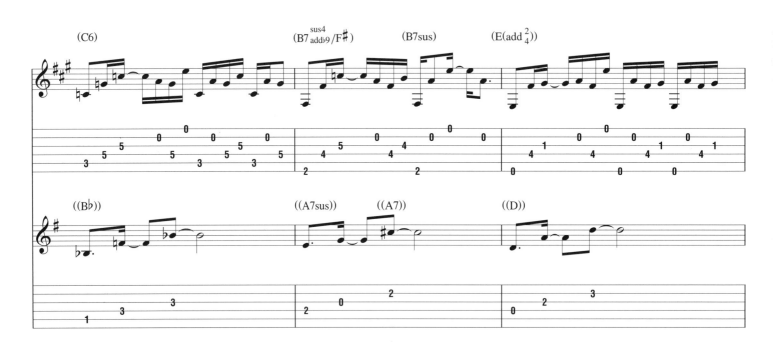
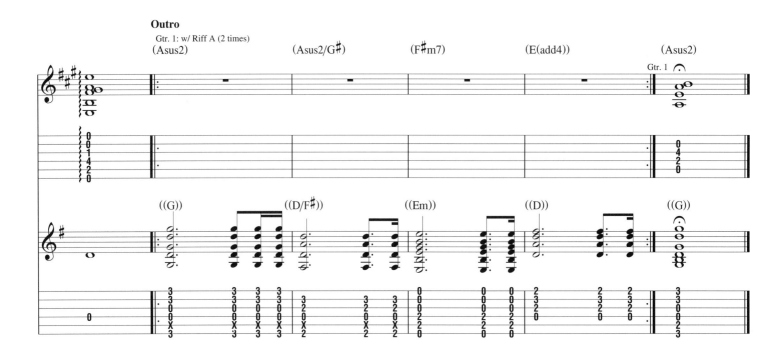

HOPE ALONE
(Guitar Parts)

Words and Music by
Emily Saliers and Annie Roboff

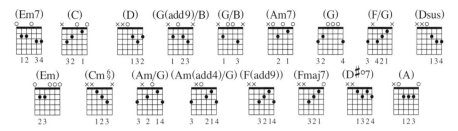

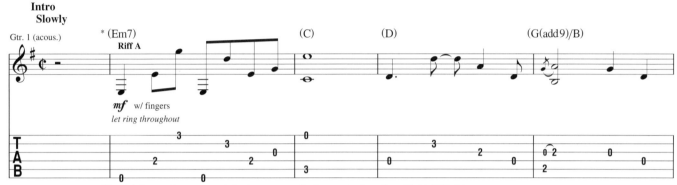

*Symbols in parentheses represent chord names respective to capoed guitars. Capoed fret is "0" in tab.

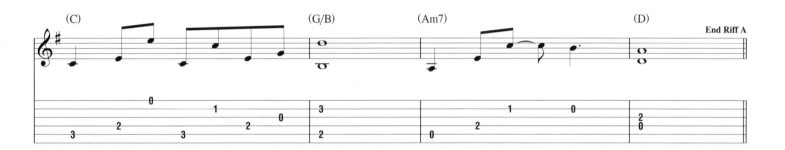

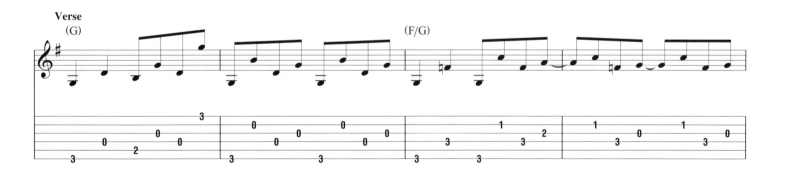

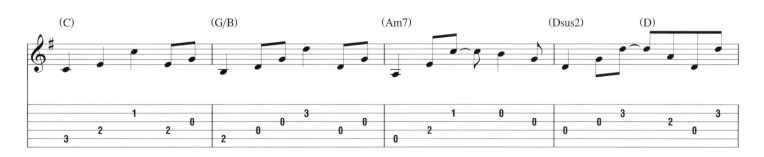

© 2002 EMI Virgin Songs, Inc. and GODHAP MUSIC, ALMO MUSIC CORP. and ANWA MUSIC
All Rights for GODHAP MUSIC Controlled and Administered by EMI VIRGIN SONGS, INC.
All Rights for ANWA MUSIC Controlled and Administered by ALMO MUSIC CORP.
All Rights Reserved   International Copyright Secured   Used by Permission

BITTERROOT
(Guitar Parts)

Words and Music by Amy Ray

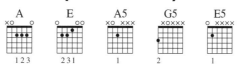

Gtr. 1: Open E tuning:
(low to high) E-B-E-G#-B-E

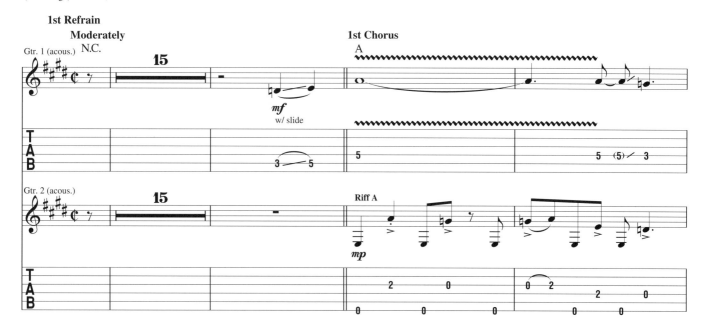

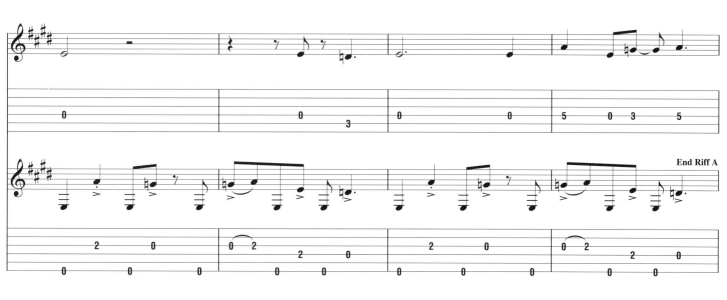

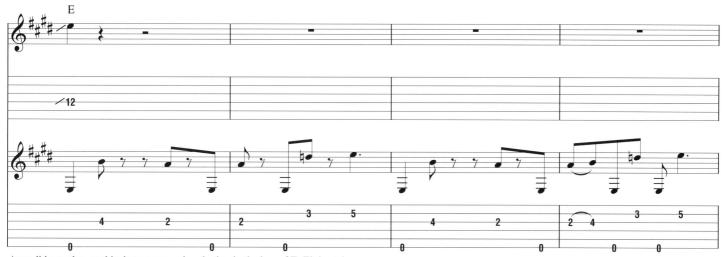

Amy did not play on this, but you can play rhythm in the key of E, Elvis style.

© 2002 EMI Virgin Songs, INC. and GODHAP MUSIC
All Rights Controlled and Administered by EMI Virgin Songs, INC.
All Rights Reserved   International Copyright Secured   Used by Permission

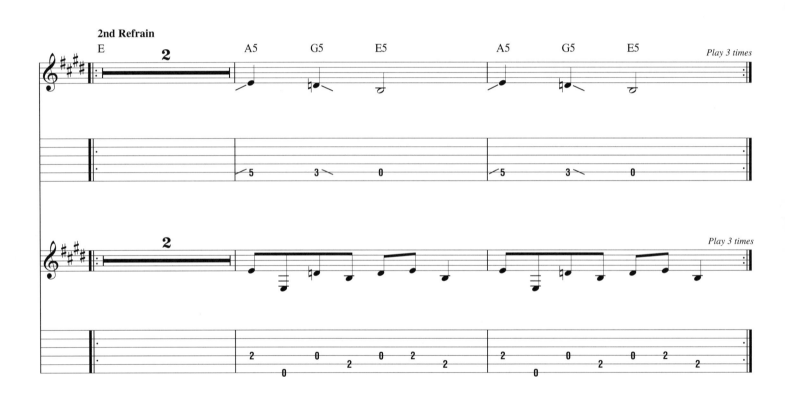
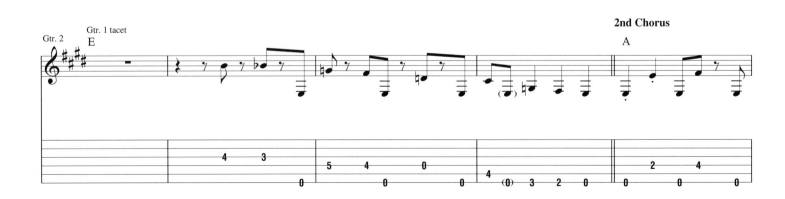

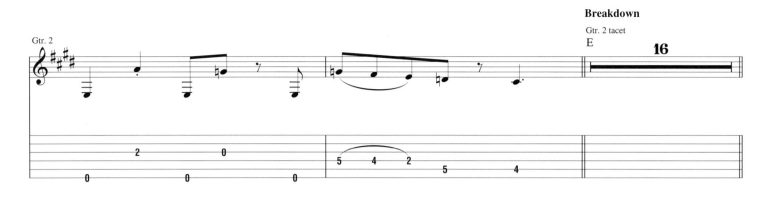
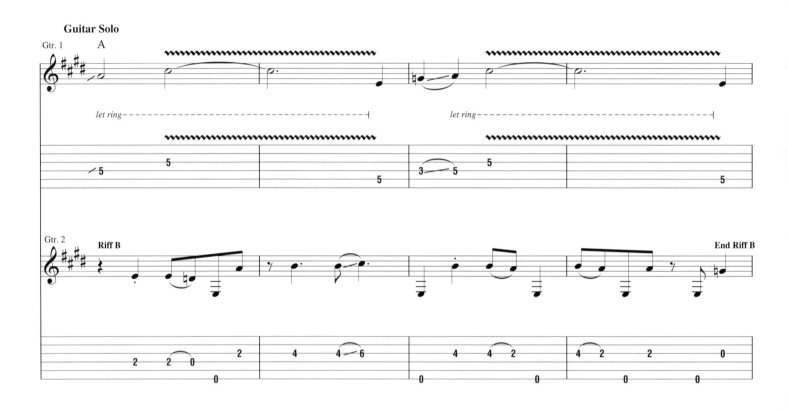

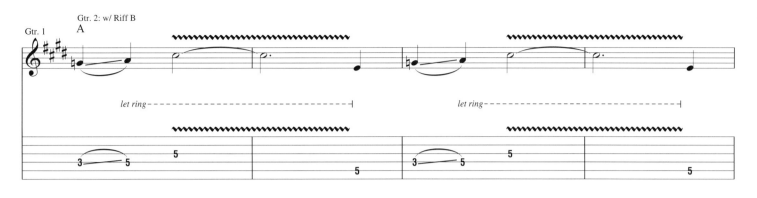
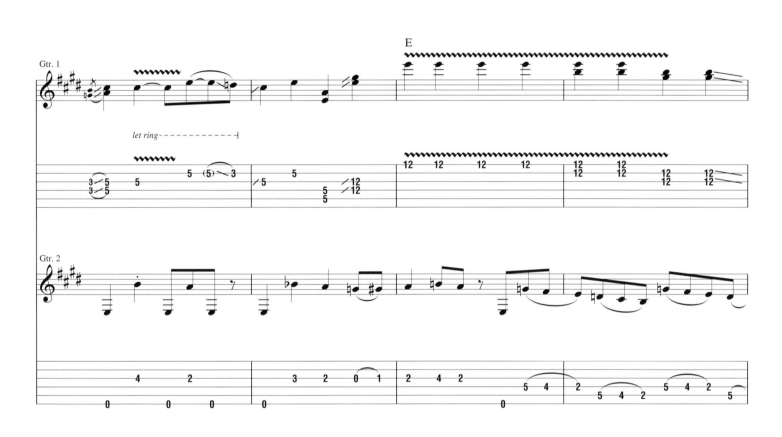
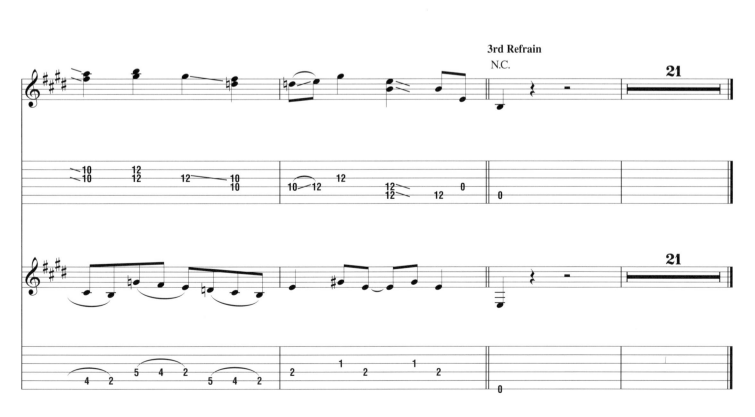

142

OUR DELIVERANCE
(Bouzouki, Mandolin & Guitar Parts)

Words and Music by Emily Saliers

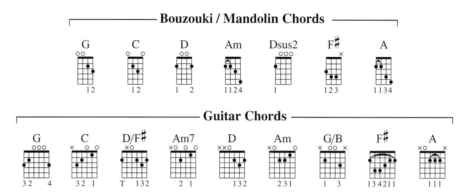

* Bouzouki tuning:
(low to high): G-D-A-E

Intro
Moderately slow

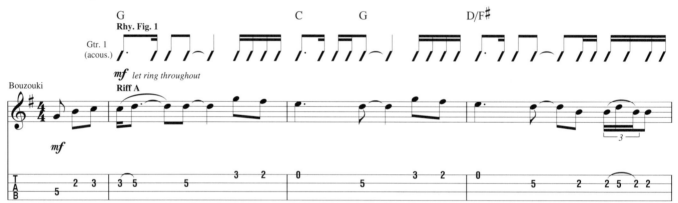

* One octave lower than Mandolin tuning.

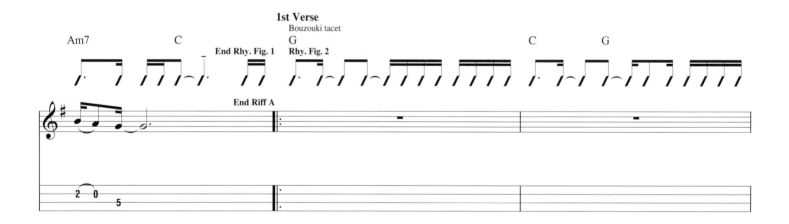

© 2002 EMI VIRGIN SONGS, INC. and GODHAP MUSIC
All Rights Controlled and Administered by EMI VIRGIN SONGS, INC.
All Rights Reserved   International Copyright Secured   Used by Permission

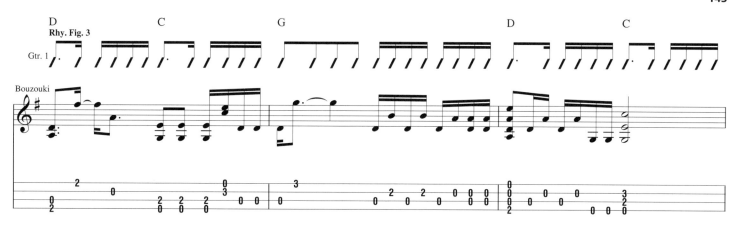
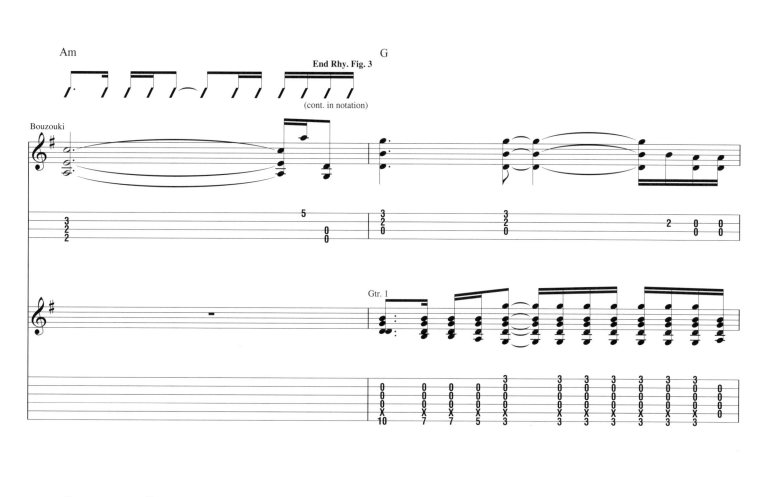
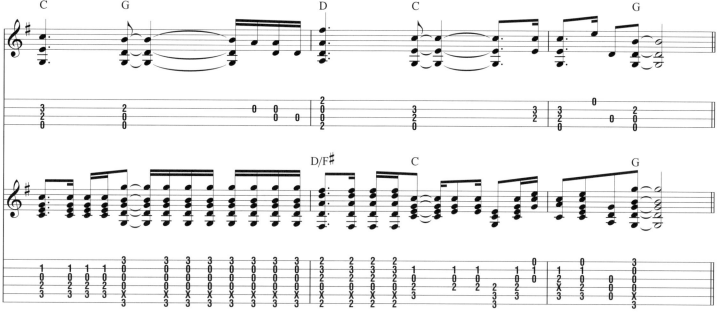

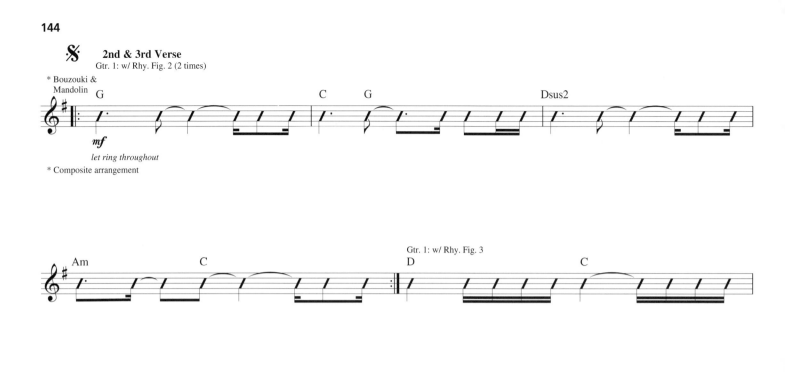
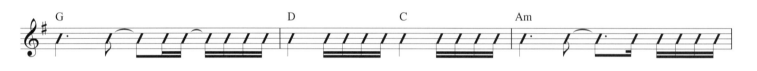
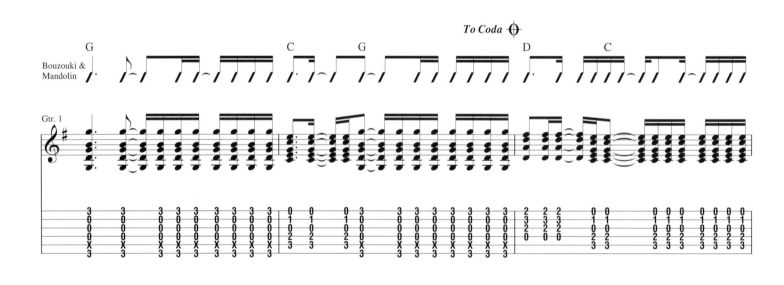
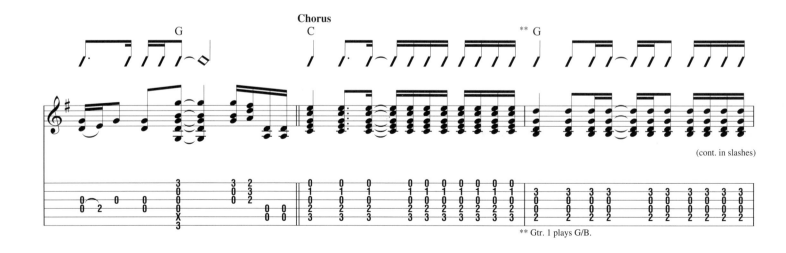

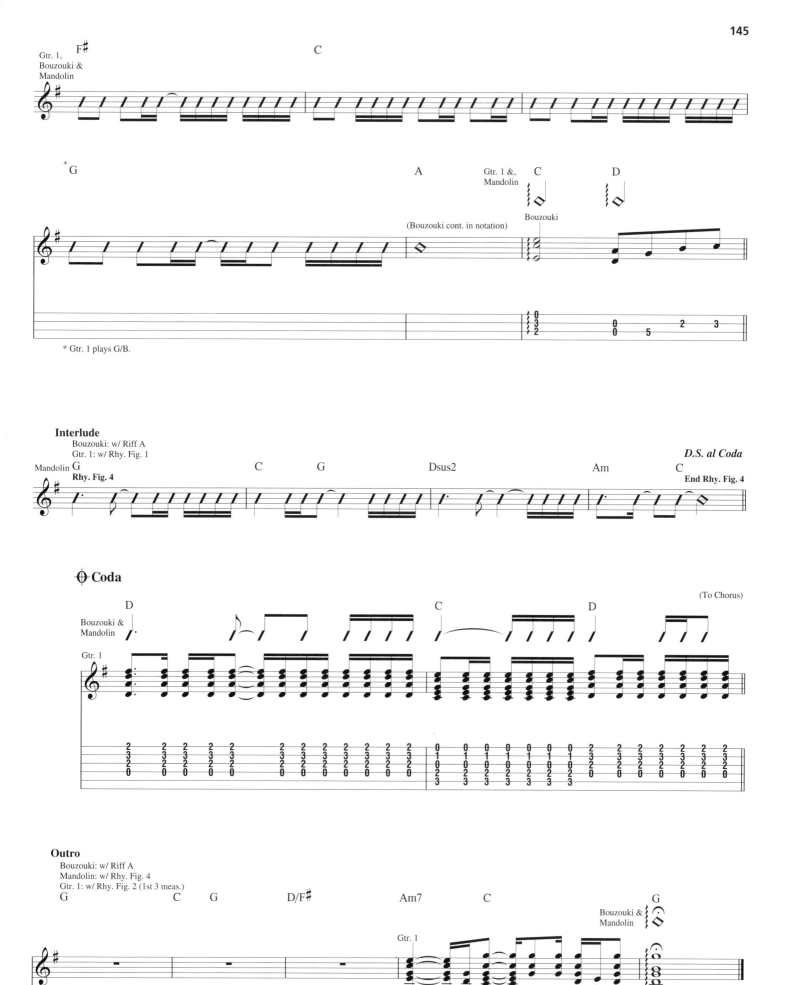

STARKVILLE
(Guitar Parts)

Words and Music by Amy Ray

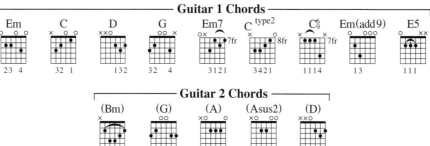

Gtr. 1: tune down 1/2 step:
(low to high) Eb-Ab-Db-Gb-Bb-Eb
Gtr. 2: Capo IV

Intro
Moderately

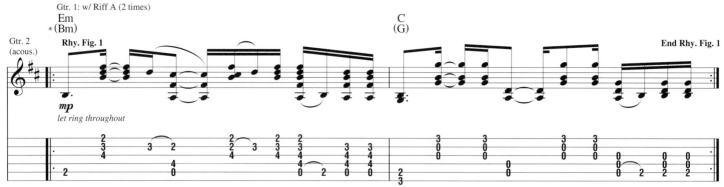

* Symbols in parentheses represent chord names respective to capoed guitar. Capoed fret is "0" in tab.

1st Verse

© 2002 EMI VIRGIN SONGS, INC. and GODHAP MUSIC
All Rights Controlled and Administered by EMI VIRGIN SONGS, INC.
All Rights Reserved   International Copyright Secured   Used by Permission

NUEVAS SENORITAS
(Mandolin & Guitar Parts)

Words and Music by Amy Ray

© 2002 EMI VIRGIN SONGS, INC. and GODHAP MUSIC
All Rights Controlled and Administered by EMI VIRGIN SONGS, INC.
All Rights Reserved   International Copyright Secured   Used by Permission

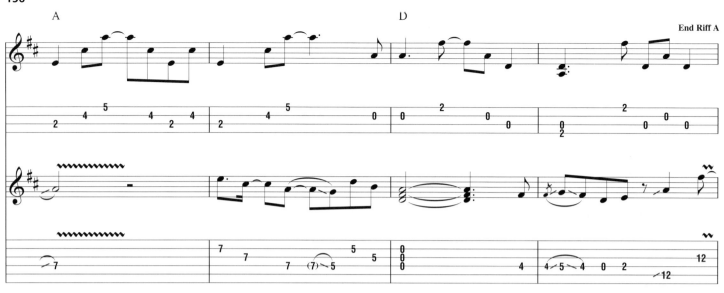
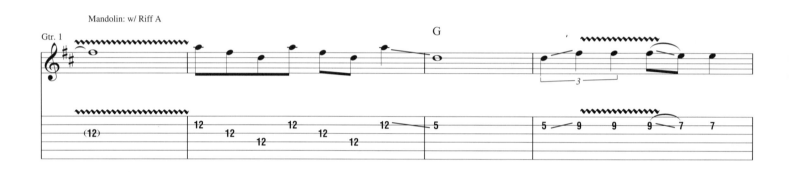
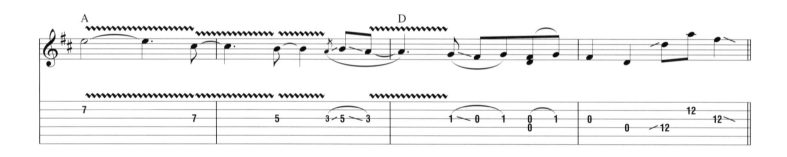
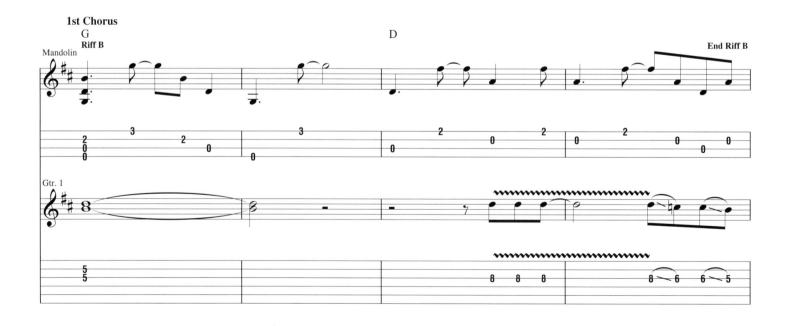

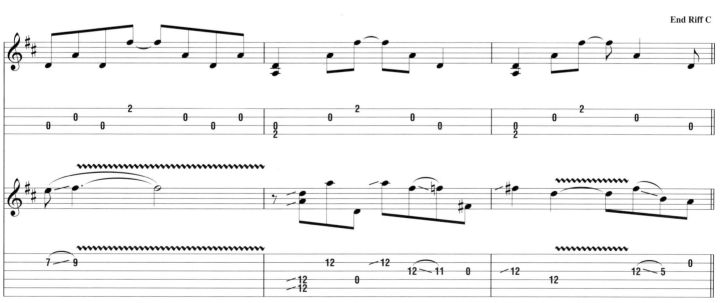

2nd Verse

Mandolin: w/ Riff A (2 times)

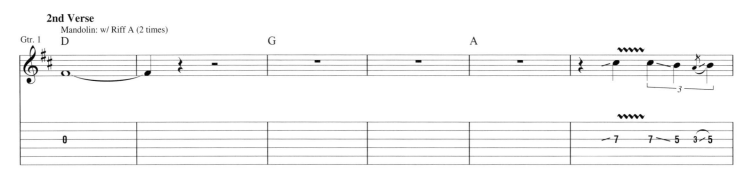

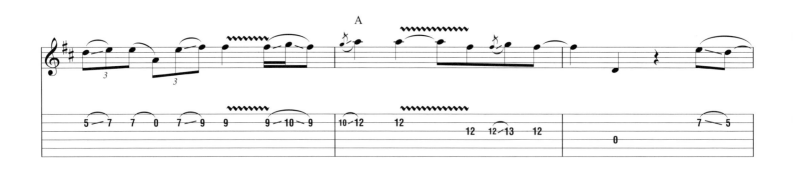

2nd Chorus

Mandolin: w/ Riff B (3 times)

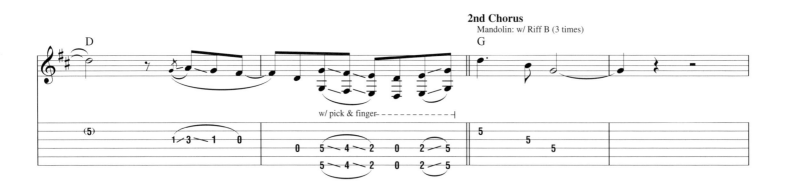

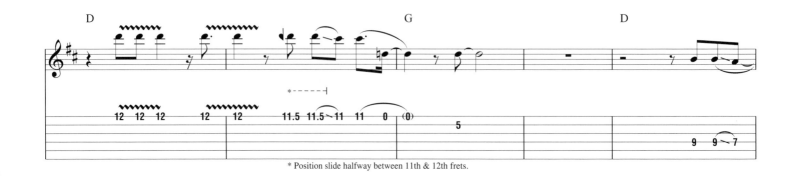

*Position slide halfway between 11th & 12th frets.

2nd Interlude

Guitar Solo

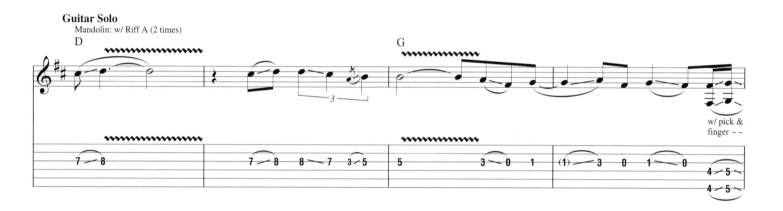

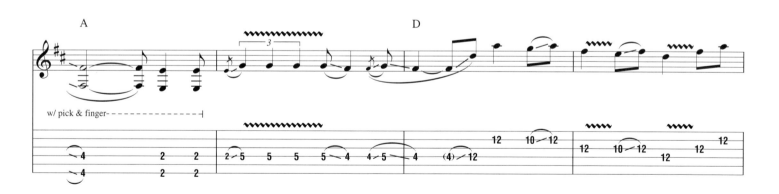

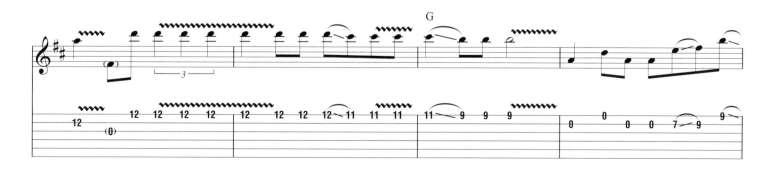

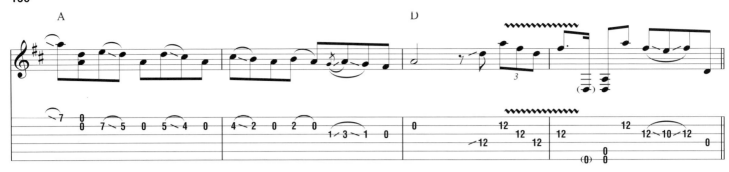

3rd Chorus
Mandolin: w/ Riff B (2 1/2 times)

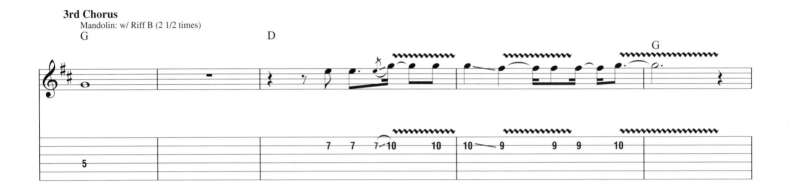